BTS

Test Your
Super–Fan Status

STERLING CHILDREN'S BOOKS
New York

An Imprint of Sterling Publishing
1166 Avenue of the Americas
New York, NY 10036

ISBN 978-1-4549-3479-0

For information about custom editions, special sales, and premium and corporate purchases, please contact Sterling Special Sales at 800-805-5489 or specialsales@ sterlingpublishing.com.

Manufactured in the United Kingdom
Lot #:
2 4 6 8 10 9 7 5 3 1
10/18

sterlingpublishing.com

Interior design by Derrian Bradder
Cover design by Angie Allison

Photo credits
Front cover: Yonhap News Agency/
Press Association Images
Page 1: Frazer Harrison/Getty Images
Page 2: Jeff Kravitz/Getty Images
Pages 3-5: Frazer Harrison/Getty Images
Page 6: Kevin Mazur/Getty Images
Page 7: Frazer Harrison/Getty Images
Page 8: Yonhap News Agency/
Press Association Images
Stock photography from www.shutterstock.com

BTS

Test Your
Super-Fan Status

Written by Kate Hamilton
Edited by Helen Brown

STERLING CHILDREN'S BOOKS
New York

CONTENTS

ABOUT THIS BOOK

RM, JIN, SUGA, J-HOPE, JIMIN, V, AND JUNGKOOK

The seven-member group BTS, also known as Bangtan Boys, are the biggest band in the world right now.

They burst onto Korea's pop scene in 2013, and five years later dropped their third album, *Love Yourself: Tear*, which debuted at Number One on the US *Billboard* 200. They became the first K-Pop group to achieve a Number One album in the USA, and in 2018 topped the charts for the second time with *Love Yourself: Answer*, earning their place as a global sensation.

Hugely interactive on social media with their fans, who they proudly call ARMY, you may think you know everything about BTS. So, are you ready to be tested on your trivia knowledge with fun quizzes and puzzles, and to let your imagination run wild with fascinating stories to fill in?

Well, of course you are! Grab a pen and follow the instructions at the top of each page—you can check your answers on **pages 91 to 96**. Get clued up on the Kings of K-Pop and discover what sort of BTS fan you really are.

ARE YOU THEIR NO. 1 FAN?

SO, YOU THINK YOU KNOW ALL ABOUT THE BTS BOYS? TAKE THIS QUIZ TO FIND OUT HOW MUCH OF A FAN YOU REALLY ARE. CHECK YOUR ANSWERS ON **PAGE 91**.

1. What is J-Hope's favorite color?
   a. Gold
   b. Blue
   c. Green

2. Who won the gold medal in the *Run BTS!* V-Live video dog challenge called "Pet Friends"?
   a. Jin
   b. RM
   c. J-Hope

3. RM is nicknamed the God of ....
   a. War
   b. Peace
   c. Destruction

4. ARMY is an acronym for "Adorable .... MC for Youth"?

a. Representative

b. Role

c. Radical

5. Bang Si-hyuk, who brought BTS together, has earned which nickname?

a. Legend

b. Hitman

c. Mr. Big

6. Who do the boys say is the best cook in the group?

a. V

b. Jin

c. Jungkook

7. RM said that he learned English by watching which television show?

a. *Friends*

b. *SpongeBob SquarePants*

c. *The Simpsons*

8. When an interviewer asked who in the group is the funniest, the BTS boys all pointed at one person. Who?

a. Suga

b. Jimin

c. Jungkook

9. Jin is nicknamed what by the others?

    a. Dad

    b. Granny

    c. Auntie

10. J-Hope's autograph includes a sketch of an object. What is it?

    a. Tree

    b. Flower

    c. Bee

11. Who did Suga say were his favorite boy band?

    a. One Direction

    b. Backstreet Boys

    c. NSYNC

12. In the video for the single "Dope", what costume was Jungkook wearing?

    a. Fireman

    b. Soldier

    c. Police Officer

FACT FILE: RM

ONLY THREE OF THESE FOUR STATEMENTS ABOUT RM ARE TRUE. PUT A CHECK IN THE BOX BESIDE EACH STATEMENT THAT YOU THINK IS TRUE, AND A CROSS IF IT'S A LIE. THE ANSWERS ARE ON **PAGE 91**.

☐ **1.** RM's favorite food is meat of any kind.

☐ **2.** RM keeps two dollars in his pocket as a lucky charm.

☐ **3.** RM thinks his feet are ugly.

☐ **4.** RM can do a great impression of Marge Simpson from *The Simpsons*.

FIND THE TUNE

EVERYWHERE YOU LOOK—UP, DOWN, FORWARDS, BACKWARDS, AND EVEN DIAGONALLY—ALL YOU SEE IS BTS AND THEIR HIT SONGS. CAN YOU FIND THE TWELVE SONG TITLES THAT BELONG TO THE WORLD OF BTS? IF YOU GET STUCK, TURN TO **PAGE 91.**

"FIRE"

"SAVE ME"

"NO MORE DREAM"

"SILVER SPOON"

"FAKE LOVE"

"SPRING DAY"

"MIC DROP"

"DANGER"

"WAR OF HORMONE"

"DNA"

"DOPE"

"BOY IN LUV"

F	M	O	T	W	U	H	K	S	E	C	P	R	L	D
B	R	M	E	N	O	M	R	O	H	F	O	R	A	W
P	C	J	A	G	I	S	T	G	U	Y	H	E	P	S
R	U	S	X	E	M	I	C	D	R	O	P	V	I	N
N	P	H	E	F	R	D	O	X	A	J	A	W	T	E
S	M	Y	E	A	R	D	R	S	F	N	M	D	Z	R
D	J	O	V	K	L	U	E	B	D	V	G	I	S	I
B	W	Z	O	E	T	O	X	R	Y	T	A	E	P	F
I	S	I	L	V	E	R	S	P	O	O	N	R	R	K
T	C	G	E	P	R	I	D	F	B	M	K	P	I	D
M	S	J	K	H	O	W	E	P	D	E	O	Z	N	B
L	E	A	A	T	K	V	G	O	B	I	N	G	O	
N	N	O	F	Y	R	I	P	S	P	U	T	W	D	R
L	W	S	A	V	E	M	E	C	E	H	I	L	A	C
N	R	E	V	U	L	N	I	Y	O	B	D	J	Y	P

CELEBRITY LOVE

ARMY IS RECRUITING MORE AND MORE STAR FANS TO ITS RANKS! BELOW IS A LIST OF COMMENTS OR TWEETS CELEBRITIES HAVE MADE ABOUT THE BOYS. TAKE A LOOK AT THE NAMES BELOW AND TRY TO MATCH THE CELEB WITH THE QUOTE. THEN TURN TO **PAGE 92** FOR THE ANSWERS.

ANSEL ELGORT	JOHN CENA	SHAWN MENDES
BACKSTREET BOYS	JOHN LEGEND	TAYLOR SWIFT
CAMILA CABELLO	KEHLANI	THE CHAINSMOKERS
CHARLIE PUTH	LIAM PAYNE	TYRA BANKS
HALSEY	MEGHAN TRAINOR	
JARED LETO	PETER CROUCH	

1. "They can all perform solo great. They have so many different styles. I think they would be a really tough group to be in because of their military thing with dancing. I actually really wanted to do something with them earlier on, but someone else kind of beat me to it, so I kind of backed out."

Answer: ....

2. "They're the One Direction of K-Pop. I'm down for working with them! You think I'm not down? I'm down! BTS hit me up!"

Answer: ....

3. "They r soooo sweet."

Answer: ....

4. "J-Hope is my favorite, just because he's got a little street cred like myself."

Answer: ....

5. "I'm a big fan of @bts."

Answer: ....

6. "BTS. So great meeting you!! You're killing it!!"

Answer: ....

7. "Backstage at the #BBMAs2018 with @BTS_twt."

Answer: ....

8. "Love these guys @bts_twt great performance. See you at the After."

Answer: ....

9. Meeting @BTS_twt is ... Better. Than. Smizing."

Answer: ....

10. "We are such huge fans of @BTS_twt! #BTSB #DontGoBreakingMyHeart #FakeLove."

Answer: ....

11. "That look in my eyes is love for BTS."

Answer: ....

12. "I think they're incredible. They were so sweet. They were probably the most beautiful guys I've ever seen in my life."

Answer: ....

13. "Ok i just met @BTS_twt and they are the coolest! WOW."

Answer: ....

14. "Rap Monster getting love from ... "

Answer: ....

15. "I think [BTS] are a fantastic band and I want to meet them in person one day."

Answer: ....

16. "Much♥ they are really the nicest dudes, @BTS_twt. Thanks for coming and supporting #BabyDriver. I can't wait to hear your album guys."

Answer: ....

DREAMS CAN COME TRUE

YOU ARE LUCKY ENOUGH TO BE SPENDING A DAY WITH ALL SEVEN BTS BOYS! WHAT WOULD YOU DO TOGETHER? READ THE STORY BELOW AND FILL IN THE BLANKS AS YOU GO. USE YOUR IMAGINATION TO CREATE YOUR DREAM DAY.

BTS certainly know how to lay on an arrival. At the airport, you feel excited when an assistant leads you toward a

waiting ....

Stepping inside is just as exciting, with thick carpets, twinkling fairy-lights, and a huge bar with a fridge full of drinks and snacks.

"Help yourself to whatever you would like to drink and eat," the assistant says, smiling.

You go to the fridge and take out a .... and grab

a .... to eat.

Then, sitting back in a large, soft, white leather seat, you are transported to BTS' apartment like a star. It's so luxurious that you are a little disappointed when the journey ends.

The door is opened for you, but just as you're about to step out, you have the surprise of your life. All seven members of BTS are joining you for the ride!

"You must be .... ," they say. They smile and hold their hands in the air like fists. RM explains that each of the boys is holding a piece of paper with a different day's activity on it. You get to choose which one.

You look at each of their smiling faces and then choose

....

Opening the folded piece of paper you read that it says

....

....

This is going to be such fun. Sit back and enjoy the ride because now you have BTS to keep you company!

On arrival, you all get out and see ....

It looks ....

RM says, " ....

...."

You can't wait. You say, " ....

...."

It's a great thrill when ....
....

Suga makes you laugh when ....
....

And then V ....
....

The highlight is when ....
....

You even manage to ....
....

Afterward they take you to a beautiful restaurant
overlooking the water and from the menu you order
.... , followed by .... and
ending with a delicious .... Yum!

Jimin says that his favorite food is .... and you
tell him that yours is ....

After the meal .... moves away from the table
and you carry on chatting with the others. Then, to your
surprise, music starts playing and .... walks
over to you with a mic in his hand.

He starts singing .... just for you!

When he asks if you would like to join in you laugh and say,

....

J-Hope asks what career you are interested in. You tell him

....

....

....

At the end of the perfect day, Jin presents you with a

.... on behalf of BTS, thanking you
for your company.

Before you are whisked away, you are curious about what
other activities were written on the other pieces of paper.

The boys laugh and then show you. Each one says ....

....

....

....

....

....

....

....

FACT FILE:
JIN

ONLY THREE OF THESE FOUR STATEMENTS ABOUT JIN ARE TRUE. PUT
A CHECK IN THE BOX BESIDE EACH STATEMENT THAT YOU THINK IS
TRUE, AND A CROSS IF IT'S A LIE. CHECK YOUR ANSWERS ON **PAGE 92**.

☐ **1.** When Jin joined the band he was wearing light
green underwear. Since that day he only wears
"lucky" undies in that color.

☐ **2.** Jin likes to collect *Super Mario* action figures.

☐ **3.** Jin usually wakes two hours earlier than the others.

☐ **4.** Jin wants his firstborn child to be a daughter and
his second a son.

WHO SAID IT?

BTS ALWAYS HAVE PLENTY TO SAY—EVEN IF MUCH OF IT DESCENDS INTO GIGGLES AND NONSENSE! BUT THAT'S WHY WE LOVE THEM SO MUCH. READ THE QUOTES FROM THE BTS BOYS AND FILL IN WHO SAID EACH ONE. TURN TO **PAGE 92** TO SEE IF YOU GOT IT RIGHT.

1. "I would like to be three centimetres taller."

Who said it? ....

2. "For real, I want to have wide shoulders like Jin."

Who said it? ....

3. "Anxiety and loneliness seem to be with me for life."

Who said it? ....

4. "If you don't work hard, there won't be good results."

Who said it? ....

5. "If I'm fire, J-Hope is water. He's good at 'turning off' my bad habits. He's really sociable so he's good at mixing with others and our group members."

Who said it? ....

6. "Living without passion is like being dead."

Who said it? ....

7. "First, there's V. I'm not kidding, he'll be sitting in the dorms, then suddenly he'll run around going, 'Ho! Ho! Ho!' He's really weird."

Who said it? ....

8. "We're just getting started. There are more amazing things to accomplish."

Who said it? ....

SPOT THE FAKES

READ THESE STATEMENTS ABOUT BTS, THEN DECIDE IF THEY ARE
TRUE OR FALSE. CHECK THE BOXES TO MARK YOUR ANSWERS,
THEN TURN TO **PAGE 92** TO FIND OUT HOW YOU DID.

1. During a performance of "We Are Bulletproof Pt. 2"
Jin's trousers fell down when he jumped up.

☐ True   ☐ False

2. Jungkook needs to get a watch because he is always
asking people what the time is.

☐ True   ☐ False

3. For a reason he can't explain, Jimin finds clothes pegs
hilarious.

☐ True   ☐ False

4. Jin can open a bag of candy and take off his socks
without using his hands.

☐ True   ☐ False

5. RM says he will never learn to drive in case he crashes.

☐ True   ☐ False

6. While on a promotional tour of Japan in 2014, Suga's appendix burst.

☐ True ☐ False

7. J-Hope is nicknamed "Mother" by the other bandmates because he cleans their rooms and even tells them off like a parent.

☐ True ☐ False

8. They call Suga "Grandpa," as he's the one who changes the lightbulbs, fixes doorknobs, and generally mends the things RM breaks. He is also frequently found having a nap!

☐ True ☐ False

9. At high school, J-Hope claims to have been well behaved, but he probably had little choice as his father was an English teacher at the same school.

☐ True ☐ False

10. Jimin wanted to be a chef when he was younger.

☐ True ☐ False

11. V is scared of jellyfish as he once got stung by one while on vacation.

☐ True   ☐ False

12. Jin describes himself as the "master of hide-and-seek."

☐ True   ☐ False

13. The others often say V is like an "alien."

☐ True   ☐ False

14. Jungkook doesn't like bugs.

☐ True   ☐ False

15. Suga thinks his legs are nice.

☐ True   ☐ False

MYSTERY TWEETER

ALL SEVEN BOYS ARE FANS OF THE SOCIAL-NETWORKING SITE TWITTER. CAN YOU GUESS WHICH BAND MEMBER POSTED THE FOLLOWING TWEETS? WRITE YOUR ANSWER AT THE BOTTOM OF THE PAGE, THEN CHECK **PAGE 92** TO SEE IF YOU ARE RIGHT.

🐦 I miss everyone so much today.

....

🐦 A really enjoyable performance after a long time.
My hair is so funny.

....

🐦 We're off. Do anticipate a lot.

....

🐦 #VTCosmetic#CicaLine#TigerCushionCream
#TroublePatchCare#VTSunSpray

....

🐦 Remember to take your meals.

The mystery Tweeter is ....

IN THE STARS

DISCOVER WHAT YOUR STAR SIGN SAYS ABOUT YOU AND THEN SEE WHICH BAND MEMBER WOULD BE YOUR IDEAL DATE. WHY NOT COMPARE YOUR RESULTS WITH YOUR FRIENDS, TOO?

AQUARIUS (21ST JANUARY – 19TH FEBRUARY)

This is J-Hope's star sign.

Personality Traits: unassuming, honest, loyal, intelligent, artistic, poetic

You like: being active, acting, trying new things, making friends

You don't like: boredom, being uncreative

Your Ideal Day: J-Hope loves to talk and if he took you to dinner at a top-class restaurant, he would never run out of things to say!

PISCES (20TH FEBRUARY – 20TH MARCH)

This is Suga's star sign.

Personality Traits: trustworthy, creative, quiet, sensitive

You like: reading, painting, drawing, writing

You don't like: being the center of attention, parties

Your Ideal Day: A heart-to-heart with Suga as you take a romantic barefoot stroll along a moonlit beach with the water lapping at your toes.

ARIES (21ST MARCH – 20TH APRIL)

Personality Traits: strong-willed, spontaneous, ambitious, passionate, fun

You like: meeting new people, sport, adventure, outdoor activities

You don't like: staying at home, organization, board games

Your Ideal Day: J-Hope loves a laugh and would be great company at the cinema watching a comedy, even if he did laugh a little too loudly!

TAURUS (21ST APRIL – 21ST MAY)

Personality Traits: sympathetic, strong, stubborn, practical

You like: helping others, old friends, gardening, decorating, making things

You don't like: unreliable people, losing control

Your Ideal Day: Get creative with Suga by spending a day learning a new skill—pottery, glass-blowing, painting. You name it!

GEMINI (22ND MAY – 21ST JUNE)

Personality Traits: adaptable, imaginative, affectionate, charismatic, inspirational

You like: trying new experiences, parties, lively conversation

You don't like: having nothing to do, quiet, being on your own

Your Ideal Day: V loves an amusement park and he reckons it would be doubly nice holding the hand of the person he fancies on a ride!

CANCER (22ND JUNE – 23RD JULY)

Personality Traits: independent, protective, careful
You like: home life, history, cooking
You don't like: disorganization, being let down
Your Ideal Day: Jin will warm your heart by cooking you a romantic meal at his home or maybe even yours!

LEO (24TH JULY – 23RD AUGUST)

Personality Traits: natural leader, vocal, brave, dynamic
You like: being center stage, parties, fun, adventure
You don't like: indecision, being sad, lack of money
Your Ideal Day: Jimin really comes alive when he performs. Imagine him inviting you to join him center stage!

VIRGO (24TH AUGUST – 23RD SEPTEMBER)

This is RM's and Jungkook's star sign.

Personality Traits: charming, easy-going, good team player
You like: helping others, being amusing, finding new hobbies
You don't like: stubbornness, selfishness, seriousness
Your Ideal Day: RM speaks the best English in the group and would make the perfect partner to teach you Korean for those smoochy words of love!

LIBRA (24TH SEPTEMBER – 23RD OCTOBER)

This is Jimin's star sign.

Personality Traits: understanding, caring, quiet and shy
You like: being active, having fun with friends
You don't like: making decisions, being competitive
Your Ideal Day: Jimin loves a laid-back, fun date. A day at the bowling alley together would be a strike!

SCORPIO (24TH OCTOBER – 22ND NOVEMBER)

Personality Traits: bold, focused, capable, determined

You like: a good argument, keeping in touch with friends, parties

You don't like: being alone, having nothing to do

Your Ideal Day: Let artistic Jungkook express himself with pencil and paper, drawing your likeness as you pose for him, and you get to stare into his eyes for hours!

SAGITTARIUS (23RD NOVEMBER – 21ST DECEMBER)

This is Jin's star sign.

Personality Traits: intense, loyal, philosophical, lively

You like: tidiness, helping others, meaningful conversations

You don't like: lies, scattiness

Your Ideal Day: Neat and tidy, that's our Jin. He would like nothing better than to help tidy, and perhaps decorate, your room!

CAPRICORN (22ND DECEMBER – 20TH JANUARY)

This is V's star sign.

Personality Traits: intelligent, fun, persevering

You like: sharing secrets, partying, making firm friends

You don't like: injustice, surprises, inconsiderateness

Your Ideal Day: Party hard with V who loves being in the spotlight!

FACT FILE: SUGA

ONLY THREE OF THESE FOUR STATEMENTS ABOUT SUGA ARE TRUE.
PUT A CHECK IN THE BOX BESIDE EACH STATEMENT THAT YOU THINK
IS TRUE, AND A CROSS IF IT'S A LIE. CHECK YOUR ANSWERS
ON **PAGE 93**.

1. In real life Suga hates sugar.

2. Suga is a keen photographer.

3. Suga released a solo mixtape under the name of Agust D (backward it reads DT Suga, with DT standing for Daegu Town).

4. One of Suga's nickames is "Motionless Min" because when he has free days he doesn't do anything.

SHARING THE LOVE

BTS WEAR THEIR HEARTS ON THEIR SLEEVES, BUT CAN YOU COMPLETE THESE STATEMENTS BELOW? LIST THE THINGS THEY LOVE BY FILLING IN THE MISSING WORD FROM THE LIST OF WORDS ON **PAGE 33**. THEN CHECK OUT THE ANSWERS ON **PAGE 93**.

1. **RM**

   "If you know and feel this moment truthfully with the heart, and that you're ready to accept the moment, then from the time when you're born, the entire life can be

   .... "

2. **JIMIN**

   " .... is always fun!"

3. **V**

   "I really like looking at the work of painters and photographers from the ...."

4. JUNGKOOK

"Applying .... after a shower in the evening."

5. JIN

"Getting praised for my .... face."

6. JUNGKOOK

"Playing .... games as soon as I open my eyes in the morning."

7. RM

"When I feel I am ...."

8. RM

"Midday in Seoul .... where not many people are around."

9. JUNGKOOK

"Going to any .... to drink alone."

10. JIN

"When members are laughing at my ...."

11. SUGA

"Going to .... late when having a day off."

12. J-HOPE

"Completely .... my hair after a shower."

13. V

"I think it's really pretty when girls wear wide

...."

BEAUTIFUL	JOKES
BED	LOVED
COMPUTER	PANTS
CREAM	PAST
DRYING	RESTAURANT
FOREST	TRAVELING
HANDSOME	

CRACK THAT CROSSWORD

READ THE CLUES BELOW AND PLACE YOUR ANSWERS IN THE CROSSWORD GRID ON THE OPPOSITE PAGE. CHECK OUT THE ANSWERS ON **PAGE 93** WHEN YOU'RE DONE.

ACROSS

2. Name of BTS' album, *2 Cool for* _ _ _ _ _ (5)

4. BTS also stands for _ _ _ _ _ _ _ _ _ _ _ Boy Scouts (11)

5. The group's management, _ _ _ Hit Entertainment (3)

6. BTS met top US singer _ _ _ _ _ _ Swift at the Billboard Music Awards (6)

DOWN

1. Name of their debut song (2, 4, 5)

3. Jin appeared in the television survival show *Law of the* _ _ _ _ _ _ (6)

5. _ _ _ _ Si-hyuk made sure the boys' career started explosively (4)

AUDITION TIME: DANCING

ROUND 1

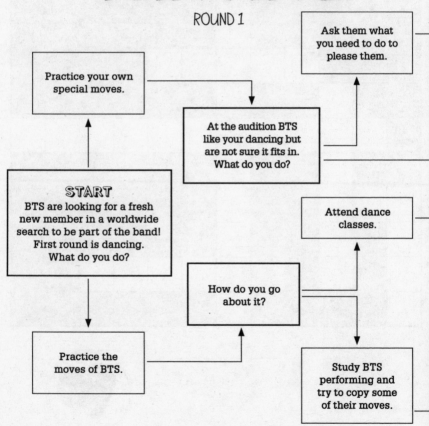

Ask them what you need to do to please them.

Practice your own special moves.

At the audition BTS like your dancing but are not sure it fits in. What do you do?

START
BTS are looking for a fresh new member in a worldwide search to be part of the band! First round is dancing. What do you do?

Attend dance classes.

How do you go about it?

Practice the moves of BTS.

Study BTS performing and try to copy some of their moves.

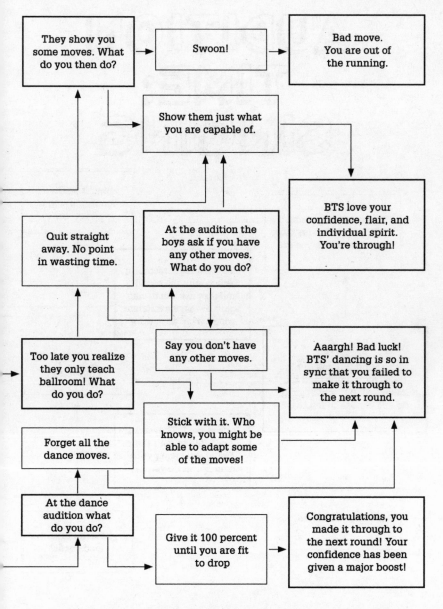

They show you some moves. What do you then do? → Swoon! → Bad move. You are out of the running.

Show them just what you are capable of.

BTS love your confidence, flair, and individual spirit. You're through!

Quit straight away. No point in wasting time.

At the audition the boys ask if you have any other moves. What do you do?

Too late you realize they only teach ballroom! What do you do?

Say you don't have any other moves.

Aaargh! Bad luck! BTS' dancing is so in sync that you failed to make it through to the next round.

Forget all the dance moves.

Stick with it. Who knows, you might be able to adapt some of the moves!

At the dance audition what do you do?

Give it 100 percent until you are fit to drop

Congratulations, you made it through to the next round! Your confidence has been given a major boost!

AUDITION TIME: SINGING

ROUND 2

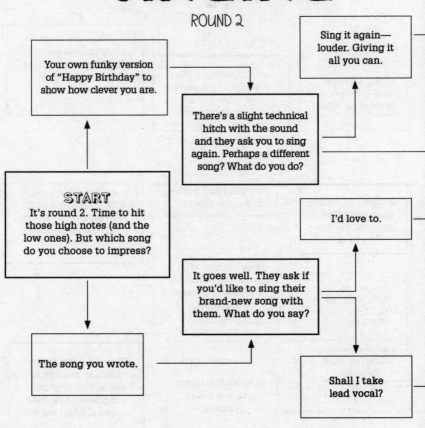

Sing it again—louder. Giving it all you can.

Your own funky version of "Happy Birthday" to show how clever you are.

There's a slight technical hitch with the sound and they ask you to sing again. Perhaps a different song? What do you do?

START
It's round 2. Time to hit those high notes (and the low ones). But which song do you choose to impress?

I'd love to.

It goes well. They ask if you'd like to sing their brand-new song with them. What do you say?

The song you wrote.

Shall I take lead vocal?

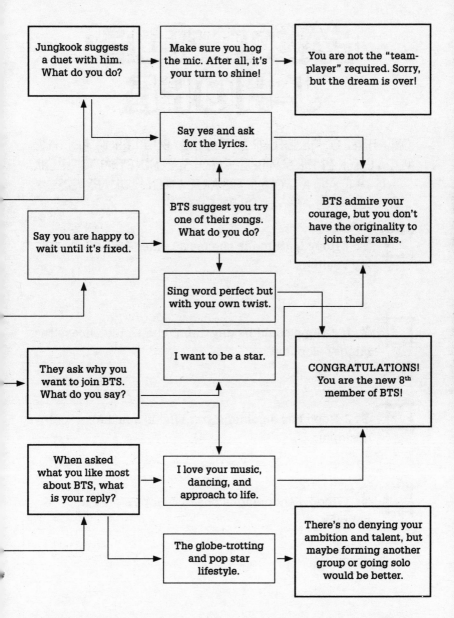

Jungkook suggests a duet with him. What do you do?

Make sure you hog the mic. After all, it's your turn to shine!

You are not the "team-player" required. Sorry, but the dream is over!

Say yes and ask for the lyrics.

BTS suggest you try one of their songs. What do you do?

BTS admire your courage, but you don't have the originality to join their ranks.

Say you are happy to wait until it's fixed.

Sing word perfect but with your own twist.

They ask why you want to join BTS. What do you say?

I want to be a star.

CONGRATULATIONS! You are the new 8th member of BTS!

When asked what you like most about BTS, what is your reply?

I love your music, dancing, and approach to life.

The globe-trotting and pop star lifestyle.

There's no denying your ambition and talent, but maybe forming another group or going solo would be better.

FACT FILE: J-HOPE

ONLY THREE OF THESE FOUR STATEMENTS ABOUT J-HOPE ARE TRUE. PUT A CHECK IN THE BOX BESIDE EACH STATEMENT THAT YOU THINK IS TRUE, AND A CROSS IF IT'S A LIE. CHECK YOUR ANSWERS ON **PAGE 93.**

1. J-Hope featured in the music video for Drake's "In My Feelings."

2. If J-Hope could be any animal he would choose the mighty elephant.

3. J-Hope has an older sister who is a fashion designer.

4. Window shopping is one of J-Hope's favorite hobbies.

A DAY IN THE LIFE

WOW! YOU AND A FRIEND HAVE WON A COMPETITION TO SPEND A DAY WITH BTS AT THEIR LUXURY APARTMENT IN SOUTH KOREA! COMPLETE THE DIARY BELOW DETAILING THIS INCREDIBLE DAY IN YOUR LIFE BY FILLING IN THE BLANKS.

Wow! What a prize. Choosing which friend to do something with is always tricky but I knew there was only really one and that was ....

When I phoned with the news, I couldn't help laughing at .... reaction.

.... 's favorite member of BTS is .... , and mine is ....

On the big day, all the transport, accommodation, food, and drink was laid on for us and we were accompanied by a friendly lady who took care of us. We stayed the night in a luxury hotel in South Korea, and then were taken in a taxi cab to the BTS apartment!

I was wearing .... , along with my

.... and my new ....

On arrival we were startled to see seven BTS boys waiting outside, beaming at us as we stepped out of the taxi. RM stepped forward and said, " ....

...."

He then introduced us to each member of the band—as if we didn't know who was who! They politely ....

....

We waited until they showed us inside, and we were so excited to have a look around!

On the walls we could see ....

....

Jin made us laugh when he said, " ....

...."

"This is Suga's room," said RM and he opened the door so we could walk in. It looked ....

There were .... and .... everywhere!

Suga said, "...

...."

Next up was V's room. It looked quite different because
.... , and it had ....

....

I asked V, " .... ,"
and he replied, " ...."

Jungook added, " ...."

J-Hope's room had ....
RM's was ....

Jin's room surprised us because ....
.... , and Jungkook looked embarrassed when we
looked into his room because he had forgotten to ....

....

Jimin's room was full of games such as ....
and .... , and he eagerly asked us if
we wanted to play a game.

"Wait," said Jin. "I have cooked some .... for us
to eat." He went off and brought it back in for us, and we all
sat down to tuck in. It was .... !

After that we played a game of .... , in which
....

"We have a surprise for you," said V. "Come." He led us to a large room, facing a small stage.

"We use this as a rehearsal room. Would you like to hear our new song?"

" .... ," I said.

The boys then disappeared for a while, and when the music started up I was expecting to hear just a recording of their new song but the boys walked on to the stage and started singing and dancing!

At the end they had big grins on their faces, but ours were even bigger as we applauded like mad.

"The song is called, ... ," said J-Hope. "Do you like it?"

" .... ," we both replied together.

The day ended with an exchange of presents. I gave them each a .... , and we were delighted when the boys gave us a ....

We left feeling like it was all a dream and never really happened. But it did. And now it's recorded in my diary for me to keep and cherish forever.

MYSTERY TWEETER

READ THESE TWEETS AND SEE IF YOU CAN WORK OUT WHO POSTED THEM. WRITE YOUR ANSWER AT THE BOTTOM OF THE PAGE THEN CHECK **PAGE 93** TO SEE JUST HOW CLEVER YOU ARE.

🐦 My fringe.

....

🐦 Hahahahahahahahahahahahahaha Jung Hoseok hahahahahahahahahahaha I love you.

....

🐦 Cock-a-doodle-doo~!!

....

🐦 Thanks to all ARMYs, our 5th year anniversary today was really enjoyable! See you again at our 6th year anniversary!!

....

🐦 Go follow the sound of the pipe!!

The mystery Tweeter is ....

FACT FILE: JIMIN

ONLY THREE OF THESE FOUR STATEMENTS ABOUT JIMIN ARE TRUE. PUT A CHECK IN THE BOX BESIDE EACH STATEMENT THAT YOU THINK IS TRUE, AND A CROSS IF IT'S A LIE. CHECK YOUR ANSWERS ON **PAGE 94**.

1. Jimin firmly believes that once his life is over he will return as a bird.

2. Jimin's favorite superhero is the Hulk because he smashes everything in his way.

3. Jimin loves taking selfies on his camera.

4. Jimin thinks his eyes are the best part of his body.

NAUGHTY OR NICE?

BTS ARE GREAT FRIENDS, BUT THEY LOVE TO TEASE EACH OTHER. READ THE COMMENTS BELOW AND CHECK WHETHER YOU THINK THEY ARE BEING NAUGHTY OR NICE.

JIMIN

"V's specialty is getting all the attention from others on to him!"

☐ Naughty   ☐ Nice

J-HOPE

"Suga is a true caretaker. He's kind of a hidden leader who takes care of everyone."

☐ Naughty   ☐ Nice

RM

"Jimin is the most romantic amongst us because he likes to give presents to all the others."

☐ Naughty   ☐ Nice

JIN

"I think I am really bad at dancing ... however, Rap Monster really cannot dance!"

☐ Naughty   ☐ Nice

SUGA

"Jin is known for his short legs in BTS."

☐ Naughty   ☐ Nice

JUNGKOOK

About Jimin: "Timid, shameless, and hates losing."

☐ Naughty   ☐ Nice

JIN

"J-Hope is like a beagle puppy. At home he's really
untidy and leaves things scattered around, and
he's also clinging on to people all the time."

☐ Naughty   ☐ Nice

JIMIN

"When I first got into the dorm and I saw Rap Monster, I
thought, 'Wow! He's really a Star!' ... but not anymore."

☐ Naughty   ☐ Nice

SUGA

About V: "Everyone says this, but people with blood
type AB are either a complete genius or a complete
idiot. He's both. But sometimes he comes up
with really good ideas and surprises us."

☐ Naughty   ☐ Nice

Whose comments are the nicest? ....

SPOT THE DIFFERENCE

Can you find eight differences between the top and bottom pictures?
You can check your answers on page 94.

MYSTERY TWEETER

CAN YOU GUESS WHICH BAND MEMBER POSTED THE FOLLOWING TWEETS? WRITE YOUR ANSWER AT THE BOTTOM OF THE PAGE THEN CHECK **PAGE 94** TO SEE IF YOUR POWERS OF BTS DETECTION ARE STRONG.

🐦 I took a video, but the members said to retake it because Jungkook's not in it.

....

🐦 So I took it again. But Jin hyung said to retake it because it seemed as though he couldn't see himself....!?

....

🐦 Activities begin~!!!

....

🐦 Thank you for always believing in us and loving us for all of these 5 years. Lately, because of all of you, I'm able to live more and experience a lot. I also really love you a lot, ARMY. Happy birthdayyy to our Bangtan.

....

🐦 Good weather.

The mystery Tweeter is ....

THE BIG INTERVIEW

YOUR EXCITEMENT HAS REACHED A LEVEL YOU NEVER KNEW EXISTED ... BTS ARE PLAYING IN YOUR HOMETOWN! YOUR LOCAL NEWSPAPER HAS ASKED YOU TO INTERVIEW THEM BEFORE THEY PERFORM. THE EDITOR HAS BEEN TIPPED OFF ABOUT WHICH HOTEL THEY ARE STAYING AT. BUT WILL YOU BE ABLE TO FIND THEM AND WILL THEY BE WILLING TO TALK TO YOU? FILL IN THE BLANK SPACES WITH ONE OF THE SUGGESTED OPTIONS OR GO WILD AND WRITE WHATEVER YOU LIKE.

With your heart pumping you arrive at the Fairview Hotel. Calm down, you tell yourself. Act professional. You are not simply a fan now. You are a reporter! A man wearing a suit and hat opens the door for you with a smile. So far, so good! But once inside you wonder what to do next. You take a look around the reception. Then you hear a voice.

"May I help you?" Turning, you see a woman behind the desk looking at you. Caught off-guard, you manage to ask

....

(for the toilet / if BTS are staying here / where is the lounge)

Not quite knowing what to do next or where to go you decide to step outside the hotel and walk around the grounds. It's a nice day, after all. Perhaps BTS are sitting outside?

Turning a corner, you hear voices in the distance. As you get nearer, your heart seems to miss a beat. It's the unmistakable voice of ....
(J-Hope / Suga / a dog)

You hear the others laugh. You feel excitement rippling through your body. Then you see them. They are ....
....
(sitting at a table chatting / making each other laugh / doing dance moves / playing "rock, paper, scissors")

You tread on a twig that makes a loud snap. Before you know it, a burly security guard is by your side, guiding you in front of the boys. "This is .... ,"
he says. (a snooper / a private area / how I earn a living)

BTS are all staring at you. You feel yourself staring back, your eyes widen and your jaw drops. It's an odd moment and you realize you should say something. Taking a deep breath, you say, ...
....
(I have been asked if I can interview you / This is a dream come true to meet you / I love you)

To your relief, the boys all smile and beckon you over. You go to sit down with them, but the security guard says, ...
....
(I will have to escort you off the premisies / They are too busy / How come you get to sit with them but I never do?)

But .... (RM / Jin / Suga / J-Hope / Jimin / V / Jungkook) comes to your rescue by saying, ...
....

(Let them stay, we would be delighted to talk to them / She is our guest / Mr. Security Guard, please leave us)

You sit down and explain fully what you have been asked to do. Jin confides that he wanted to be a reporter when he was younger. You smile and say, ...
....

(I know / Did you? / Do you regret not becoming one?)

They all laugh when .... (RM / Jin / Suga / J-Hope / Jimin / V / Jungkook) says, ...
....

(Go ahead and show Jin how it's done / He loved himself too much / He took up eating instead)

To your astonishment, they listen politely to your questions and answer them truthfully. After thanking them for their time they each stand to give you a hug and you walk away in a daze.

Now write up your dream interview with BTS on the opposite page.

EXCLUSIVE INTERVIEW
WITH BTS

By

CRACK THAT CROSSWORD

READ THE CLUES BELOW AND PLACE YOUR ANSWERS IN THE CROSSWORD GRID ON THE OPPOSITE PAGE. CHECK OUT THE ANSWERS ON **PAGE 94** WHEN YOU'RE DONE.

ACROSS

1. The _ _ _ Bullet, the name of their first full-length concert (3)

3. Jin is a fan of _ _ _ _ _ West, a famous American rapper (5)

5. RM studied in New _ _ _ _ _ _ _ (7)

DOWN

2. BTS appeared on a hit US chat show hosted by Ellen _ _ _ _ _ _ _ _ _ (9)

4. Spring is the favorite season of this BTS member (5)

6. The oldest member of the group (3)

MYSTERY TWEETER

USE YOUR SLEUTHING SKILLS TO WORK OUT WHICH
BAND MEMBER POSTED THE FOLLOWING TWEETS.
WRITE YOUR ANSWER AT THE BOTTOM OF THE PAGE
THEN CHECK **PAGE 95** TO SEE HOW YOU DID.

I'll become someone who is more awesome and can be a source of strength Thank you so much, ARMY.

....

The last one's a blood moon.

....

Thank you for being with us for 5 years.
Really, thank you!

....

ARMY's guardians.

....

It's hot.

The mystery Tweeter is ....

TOUR-TIME TEASER

THE BOYS ARE KICKING OFF A MAJOR TOUR BUT A DODGY TYPIST HAS MISSPELLED THE SONG TITLES, GETTING ALL THE LETTERS MIXED UP. THE BOYS DESPERATELY NEED TO KNOW THEIR SET LIST, BUT WITH MINUTES TO SPARE THEY CAN'T WORK OUT WHAT THEY'RE SUPPOSED TO BE SINGING. CAN YOU STEP IN TO UNRAVEL THE SONG TITLES AND SAVE THE SHOW? THE ANSWERS ARE ON **PAGE 95**.

1. "ON ROME ARMED"

....

2. "EW ERA BLURTOEFLOP TP.2"

....

3. "GANDER"

....

4. "RAW OF ROOMHEN"

....

5. "YOB IN VLU"

....

6. "DOLOB, WASTE & RATES"

....

7. "RIFE"

....

8. "KEAF OLEV"

....

9. "PODE"

....

10. "AND"

....

11. "VASE EM"

....

12. "CMI PROD"

....

FACT FILE:
V

ONLY THREE OF THESE FOUR STATEMENTS ABOUT V ARE TRUE. PUT A CHECK IN THE BOX BESIDE EACH STATEMENT THAT YOU THINK IS TRUE, AND A CROSS IF IT'S A LIE. CHECK YOUR ANSWERS ON **PAGE 95**.

☐ **1.** V describes himself as being like a monkey.

☐ **2.** V was very close to his paternal grandmother who brought him up for fourteen years because his parents were busy working on their farm.

☐ **3.** V's favorite superhero is Iron Man.

☐ **4.** When V was a child, he wanted to be an astronaut.

SHHH!

HERE ARE SOME SURPRISING AND EMBARRASSING FACTS ABOUT THE BOYS THAT THEY HAVE LET SLIP AND NOW WISH THEY HADN'T! CAN YOU GUESS WHICH CRINGE-WORTHY FACT RELATES TO WHICH BAND MEMBER? WRITE A NAME BELOW EACH FACT, THEN TURN TO **PAGE 95** TO REVEAL THE ANSWERS.

1. He is said to do "strange contortions in bed."

Who was it? ....

2. He has a habit of biting his nails.

Who was it? ....

3. He has the dirtiest bed.

Who was it? ....

4. He confessed to wearing Jungkook's underwear when he was looking for them.

Who was it? ....

5. He is often found sleeping with both his arms raised above his head.

Who was it? ....

6. He's fond of stuffed toys.

Who was it? ....

7. If he had any superpower he would like to be able to talk to cars.

Who was it? ....

8. He borrowed V's earphones and said "he couldn't find them" when V asked for them back. Two months later he was seen wearing them!

Who was it? ....

9. He is too scared to watch horror movies.

Who was it? ....

10. When he was younger, he made his own chocolate for his mother on Valentine's Day. He attempted to melt lots of chocolate, but he accidently burnt it and his mother was very angry.

Who was it? ....

11. He has a habit of singing loudly at night in the dorm.

Who was it? ....

12. If he gets a day off, Jin wants this member of BTS to be his servant so he can order him around.

Who was it? ....

MYSTERY TWEETER

READ THESE TWEETS AND SEE IF YOU CAN WORK OUT WHO POSTED THEM. WRITE YOUR ANSWERS AT THE BOTTOM OF THE PAGE, THEN CHECK **PAGE 95** TO SEE IF YOU WERE RIGHT.

🐦 What are you doing?

....

🐦 I'm sorry everyone. I wanted to look at the chat window but closed it with a single click. I will answer your questions next time. Sorry and thank you !!

....

🐦 Will Monie love me ... ?

....

🐦 In the winter it's (all about) puffed rice snacks.

....

🐦 A few days ago, I asked Jungkook to cover this song so he did it the next day then sent it to me via (Kakao) talk. The moment you listen to it, it's not Jungkook, it's heaven.

The mystery Tweeter is ....

JOKER IN THE PACK

BTS ARE KNOWN FOR THEIR SILLY SENSE OF HUMOR, AND WHEN WE AREN'T LAUGHING AT THEIR ANTICS THEN *THEY* CERTAINLY ARE! BUT JUST WHO IS THE FUNNIEST? YOU CAN BE THE JUDGE! GIVE EACH FUNNY LINE A RATING FROM ONE TO FIVE, THEN ADD UP THE BOYS' SCORES TO FIND OUT WHO IS THE BIGGEST JOKER.

RM

About Suga: "He used to play tennis when he was younger and he got the bronze medal in the contest ... but there were only three players. So, congratulations."

"Jimin, you got no jams!"

JIN

"Win, lose, I don't care because at the end of the day I still have this face, so who's the real winner here?"

About Suga: "He likes being attached to his bed."

SUGA

He said that his "chat-up" line to girls was:
"You like this chain? Three dollars."

?/5

"That seagull over there has a girlfriend,
but how come I can't get one?"

?/5

J-HOPE

When reminded of how uncomfortable he was with
a snake draped across his shoulders at a trip to the
zoo, J-Hope told an interviewer: "I hate snakeu!"

?/5

"Dirty water in my faceu!"

?/5

JIMIN

About the BTS auditioning process: "I went so far as
to learn how to rap, but after they had me do it once,
they were like, 'Let's just work harder on vocals.'"

?/5

"Hey, J-Hope! Don't you think I'm hot?"

?/5

V

"My grandma loves me chubby, so I keep eating."

About Rap Monster: "In my opinion, he's 10% genius and 90% idiot."

JUNGKOOK

About Suga: "He's like a grandpa. But his passion toward music is over-flooding. He also has a lot of knowledge. But he's still a grandpa."

"I was going to the bathroom, but I can't because we won an award."

Who do you think is the funniest? ....

SPOILED FOR CHOICE

WHAT WOULD YOU DO IF YOU HAD THE CHANCE TO SPEND
SOME TIME WITH THE BOYS? TAKE A LOOK AT THE OPTIONS
BELOW. ALL YOU HAVE TO DO IS PICK YOUR PREFERRED CHOICE
FOR EACH PAIR OF OPTIONS. WHY NOT GET YOUR FRIENDS
TO HAVE A GO, TOO, AND COMPARE YOUR ANSWERS?

Would you rather ...

Have a fun tennis match with J-Hope? ☐

OR

Play basketball with Suga? ☐

Go cycling with V? ☐

OR

Take a martial arts class with Jungkook? ☐

Be taught how to dance by J-Hope? ☐

OR

How to rap by RM? ☐

Spend the day at an amusement park with all of BTS? ☐

OR

Go snorkeling with all of BTS? ☐

Be taken on a personal tour of Jimin's home town? ☐

OR

Show him around your own town? ☐

Be the band's makeup artist? ☐

OR

Be their personal hairdresser? ☐

Take a helicopter ride with J-Hope? ☐

OR

Go ice-skating with J-Hope? ☐

Have Suga write you a love song? ☐

OR

V write you a poem? ☐

Join the boys in swimming with dolphins? ☐

OR

Go paragliding with them? ☐

Enjoy a karaoke night with RM? ☐

OR

Go go-karting with RM? ☐

Go to the movies with Jungkook? ☐

OR

Have a meal in a restaurant with Jungkook? ☐

Enjoy the rides at an amusement park with V? ☐

OR

Collect shells from the beach with Suga? ☐

Sing a duet with Suga? ☐

OR

Have Suga sing only to you? ☐

Join the boys on their tour bus? ☐

OR

Go backstage at one of their gigs? ☐

Be the boys' singing coach? ☐

OR

Be their personal trainer? ☐

Go shopping for clothes with the boys? ☐

OR

Watch them at work in the recording studio? ☐

Join BTS in a silly challenge game? ☐

OR

Listen to a secret from each one of them? ☐

Be the manager of BTS? ☐

OR

Be their best friend? ☐

MYSTERY TWEETER

ALL THE BOYS LOVE TALKING TO THEIR ARMY ON TWITTER. BUT WILL YOU BE ABLE TO GUESS WHICH BAND MEMBER POSTED THE FOLLOWING TWEETS? WRITE YOUR ANSWER AT THE BOTTOM OF THE PAGE, THEN CHECK **PAGE 96** TO SEE IF YOU WERE RIGHT.

🐦 It's late, so take care while going homeee. Thank you.

....

🐦 Tired.

....

🐦 We are all ddaeng! Thank you ARMY~ Everyone has worked hard for Festa!!

....

🐦 Wait, seriously, I'm dancing better than I thought? Don't laugh Park Jiminie.

....

🐦 Thank you, I'll work even harder!!! It's such a cold day, please be careful not to catch a cold!!

The mystery Tweeter is ....

FAN LOVE

IT SEEMS LIKE BTS LOVE THEIR FANS MORE THAN ANY OTHER BAND ON THE PLANET. THEY ARE SO GRATEFUL TO ARMY AROUND THE WORLD THAT THEY NEVER STOP PRAISING AND THANKING THEM. IN THE LIST OF QUOTES BELOW, MARK HOW SWEET YOU THINK EACH ONE IS BY COLORING THE HEARTS FROM 1 TO 5.

V

"I purple you."

♡♡♡♡♡

J-HOPE

"I'm your hope, I'm your angel."

♡♡♡♡♡

V

"We are here thanks to ARMY."

♡♡♡♡♡

JUNGKOOK

After their 2018 Billboard Music Awards performance:
"To me, it was fun. There were so many ARMYs in the audience so that was encouraging. I guess I felt assured. I just let it all out after hearing their loud cheer."

♡♡♡♡♡

J-HOPE

Asked if he could do anything, be anywhere, with anyone, what would it be: "Spend the day with a fan."

RM

"The fact that we stayed true to ourselves was the biggest factor. Because we are artists who work hard to make music and create performances, so we always focus on our performances, and also, we do not slack in our communication with our fans."

JIMIN

"We wouldn't have been able to do what we wanted ... ARMY is people who we are grateful for; the people that have climbed up with us. We always say this but they are our everything."

JUNGKOOK

"We are far, far away, but we will always be together."

RM

"We are most proud of our fans. Our ARMY. They made all of this possible."

J-HOPE

"To be honest, each day is tiring and difficult, but I believe that the sole reason I can make it through is because of our ARMYs."

RM

"We feel the biggest sense of achievement when we see that even though we sing in Korean, [our fans] still understand truly what they mean, and they understand what we're saying. It's the age of new media, so they take time to translate our lyrics and our speech."

SUGA

Referring to ARMY: "I hope that we will be able to strengthen each other for a long time."

SUGA

"I gain courage because we're flying together. I'm scared of falling, but I'm not afraid of landing. Thank you for being with us. I'm always thankful, and I love you."

FACT FILE: JUNGKOOK

ONLY THREE OF THESE FOUR STATEMENTS ABOUT JUNGKOOK ARE TRUE. PUT A CHECK IN THE BOX BESIDE EACH STATEMENT THAT YOU THINK IS TRUE, AND A CROSS IF IT'S A LIE. CHECK YOUR ANSWERS ON **PAGE 96**.

☐ **1.** Jungkook's stage name was nearly "Seagull" because it is the official bird of Busan, the port city where he grew up.

☐ **2.** Jungkook's favorite animal is the zebra.

☐ **3.** Jungkook likes making travel videos.

☐ **4.** When Jungkook was younger, he wanted to become a badminton player.

HEADS IN THE CLOUDS?

WITH ALL THE SUCCESS, THERE'S A DANGER THAT THE BOYS' EGOS MIGHT GET A LITTLE INFLATED. SO, HOW ARE THEY COPING? HAVE THEY GOT THEIR FEET ON THE GROUND OR ARE THEIR HEADS IN THE CLOUDS? YOU BE THE JUDGE BY READING THE QUOTES AND THEN TICKING EITHER "GROUND" OR "CLOUDS."

1. JIN

"I think I'm worldwide handsome."

☐ Ground   ☐ Clouds

2. SUGA

"Min Suga, Genius. These words should be enough."

☐ Ground   ☐ Clouds

3. V

"Do you know why the rainbow has seven colors? Because Bangtan has seven members."

☐ Ground   ☐ Clouds

4. J-HOPE

"It doesn't matter how bright my personality is, I'm still a human. I do get stressed."

☐ Ground   ☐ Clouds

5. RM

"Life is more beautiful knowing that we've taken a loan on death. Even light is treasured more when there's darkness."

☐ Ground   ☐ Clouds

6. JIMIN

"English is not a barrier when you are as cute as me!"

☐ Ground   ☐ Clouds

7. JUNGKOOK

"My name is Jungkook ... scale is international playboy."

☐ Ground   ☐ Clouds

8. JIN

"For me, I believe the face is the ultimate factor in fashion, so I can wear anything and it'll look good."

☐ Ground   ☐ Clouds

9. SUGA

"In my next life I want to be born as a rock."

☐ Ground   ☐ Clouds

10. V

"Wherever you came from, it doesn't really matter, as long as you always stand by me."

☐ Ground   ☐ Clouds

11. J-HOPE

"I was sitting in an airplane when I was writing these verses, a first-class seat no less, and it dawned on me that I was living the glorious life I'd only dreamed about when I was young and had somehow gotten used to now. But then and now, I'm still the same person, the same J-Hope."

☐ Ground   ☐ Clouds

12. JUNGKOOK

"Effort makes you. You will regret someday if you don't do your best now. Don't think it's too late but keep working on it."

☐ Ground   ☐ Clouds

SECRET GIG

OMG! YOU'VE FOUND A V.I.P. PASS FOR A TOP-SECRET GIG BTS ARE HOLDING, BUT SOME OF THE IMPORTANT DETAILS ARE MISSING. CAN YOU SOLVE THE CLUES AND WORK OUT THE LOCATION OF THE GIG AND WHO THE SPECIAL GUEST WILL BE? YOU CAN CHECK YOUR ANSWER ON **PAGE 96**.

The gig will be held in the same city where J-Hope was born, back in 1994.

Where is it? ....

The rumor is that there will be a special guest appearing at the gig. Cross out all the "K"s, "V"s, "B"s and "X"s to find the answer.

A	K	I	R	V	A	X	B	N
X	V	G	K	A	B	E	R	X
K	D	K	B	V	N	B	V	A

Who is the mystery special guest? ....

....

HELPING HANDS

BTS ARE KNOWN FOR THEIR KINDNESS, COMPASSION, AND THEIR CHARITY WORK. SEE HOW MUCH YOU KNOW ABOUT ALL THE CHARITABLE THINGS THE BOYS HAVE BEEN INVOLVED IN BY FILLING IN THE BLANKS BELOW WITH ONE OF THE THREE OPTIONS PROVIDED. THEN TURN TO **PAGE 96** FOR THE ANSWERS.

1. In 2015, they donated over 12,000 pounds of
.... to charity at the K-Star Road opening ceremony in South Korea, the home of many K-Pop entertainment companies.
(clothes / rice / potatoes)

2. BTS officially launched a campaign called
.... to help protect and support child and teen victims of domestic and school violence as well as sexual assault around the world.
(Together Forever / Unity / Love Myself)

3. .... supported graduates of his old school, Busan Hoedong Elementary School, by covering uniform expenses from 2016 until its closure in 2018.
(RM / Jin / Suga / J-Hope / Jimin / V / Jungkook)

4. On his 25th birthday, ... donated over twenty pounds of Korean beef to 39 orphanages in Korea under the name of "ARMY."
(RM / Jin / Suga / J-Hope / Jimin / V / Jungkook)

5. BTS joined Korea's .... Challenge campaign to raise money and awareness for amyotrophic lateral sclerosis.
(Ice Bucket / Pie Face / Hula Hoop)

6. Each member of BTS donated approximately $8,000 to the 4/16 Sewol Families for Truth and A Safer Society. This was an organization connected to the families of the victims of the Sewol Ferry tragedy which happened in .... (2011 / 2013 / 2014)

7. In 2014, BTS visited a children's home and a home for the elderly to meet and talk to them and bring them food and drink as part of a program by ....
(Meet and Greet / Caring Hands / Love Food Bank)

8. .... and .... each donated personally signed shirts to the "WeAja Charity Auction" to raise money for families with little money.
(RM / Jin / Suga / J-Hope / Jimin / V / Jungkook)

MYSTERY TWEETER

BTS LOVE TALKING TO THEIR ARMY ON TWITTER. BUT WILL YOU BE ABLE TO TELL WHICH BAND MEMBER POSTED ALL OF THESE TWEETS? WRITE YOUR ANSWER AT THE BOTTOM OF THE PAGE, THEN CHECK **PAGE 96** TO SEE JUST HOW CLEVER YOU ARE!

Thank you for making it so "healing" for us. I love you.

....

Boy with pearl earrings #Hello

....

I PurpleYou I PurpleYou I PurpleYou!!! I PurpleYou!!! #ARMYheartBangtan

....

I'll run towards ARMY

....

I'll reveal him eating and jumping later on through a live broadcast on V App, have a Yeontan-full day.

The mystery Tweeter is ....

FAME GAME

DO YOU FANCY BEING PART OF A BAND THAT MIGHT ONE DAY BECOME A WORLDWIDE PHENOMENON LIKE BTS? TAKE THIS QUIZ TO DISCOVER YOUR INNER SUPERSTAR. WILL YOU BE A SMASH-HIT SINGER, A TV DIVA, OR A STAGE STARLET? CIRCLE A, B, OR C AND THEN CHECK OUT YOUR STAR STATUS AT THE END ON **PAGES 86-87**.

1. How would your friends describe you?
   a. Outgoing
   b. Quietly confident
   c. A little shy

2. What would your ideal day out involve?
   a. Thrill-seeking, white-knuckle rides at the amusement park
   b. Go-karting
   c. Scuba diving

3. What type of animal most fits your personality?
   a. Monkey
   b. Lion
   c. Panda

4. The essential requirement of your cell phone is that it is:

   a. Glittery

   b. Brightly colored

   c. In a shatterproof casing

5. What would you rather have a ride in or on?

   a. A racing car

   b. A hot-air balloon

   c. An elephant

6. Your favorite music is played at a party. What do you do?

   a. Drag everyone up on the dance floor

   b. Head to the dance floor alone

   c. Cut some moves while casually talking

7. Which words are most likely to appear on your school report?

   a. Excitable

   b. Dreamer

   c. Listener

8. If a singing coach said that you were flat, what would you do?
   a. Continue practicing
   b. Play an instrument or dance instead
   c. Be very upset

9. You win a fancy-dress competition. What would you do when you accept the award?
   a. Make an emotional speech, thanking family, friends, and anyone who knows you and made this moment possible
   b. Smile, say "thanks" and leave
   c. Modestly shrug and say that there were better outfits than yours

10. What is usually your favorite course in a restaurant?
    a. The dessert
    b. The appetizer
    c. The main

11. If your house was on fire and you had to make a run for it, what would you grab?
    a. Your cell phone
    b. Your coat
    c. Your teddy

TURN THE PAGE TO DISCOVER YOUR INNER SUPERSTAR ...

THE RESULTS

COUNT UP THE NUMBER OF "A"S, "B"S, AND "C"S YOU MARKED IN THE QUIZ ON **PAGES 83-85**. THEN READ YOUR STAR STATUS IN THE FULL ANALYSIS BELOW.

MOSTLY "A"S: SMASH-HIT SINGER

You are certainly not frightened of the spotlight. In fact, you love it! If there's a stage, there's only one place to stand, and that's the center. You have the drive, confidence, and energy to succeed, but just remember that you need to focus, work hard, and develop that talent inside you. Go for it!

MOSTLY "B"S: TV DIVA

It's not just about being the center of attention and the loudest with you, is it? You have a quieter approach and confidence in doing things how you want to do them and not just following what others do. As long as you don't alienate yourself from people then you have an excellent chance of success.

MOSTLY "C"S: STAGE STARLET

Nobody is going to accuse you of being the life and soul of the party. But would you want to be? Sensible and cautious are your watchwords, and that can hardly be the wrong approach. But if you really want to make it as a star then you will have to take some risks every now and then and be prepared to step out of the shadows. You can do it, if you really want to. But the question is, "do you?"

LIKE OR LOVE?

ARMY HAS PLENTY TO "LIKE" ABOUT THE RANDOM THINGS THAT
BTS SAY, BUT HOW MUCH DO WE "LOVE" THEIR COMMENTS?
TAKE A LOOK AT THE CUTE, THOUGHTFUL, INTERESTING, AND
AMUSING THINGS THEY HAVE SAID BELOW AND COLOR
IN EITHER THE "LIKE" CIRCLE OR THE "LOVE" HEART.
(TRY HARD NOT TO "LOVE" EVERYTHING!)

JIN

"When I eat, I feel happy and everyone looks like angels."

JUNGKOOK

"I suddenly have a lot of wrinkles near my eyes ... Maybe it's
because I smile a lot?"

SUGA

"Jungkook has a good memory so he can imitate us well.
And I remember that when Jungkook first came, he was
shorter than me. Seeing him grow taller makes me feel
like I've raised him."

JIN

"I didn't know fire could be that hot."

○ ♡

SUGA

"Cheaters never win, but I just graduated."

○ ♡

JIMIN

"I think J-Hope is awesome. And people think he's always nice and innocent, but inside his smiley face, there's an evil living there."

○ ♡

SUGA

"I think we're flying too high. I see so much, and it all seems so far away. I'm scared to look below me too."

○ ♡

JIMIN

"J-Hope winds me up all the time but never stop smiling even when he does that. But you can never punch someone who looks so happy like that."

○ ♡

RM

"Sometimes we get really depressed but in love, we should take off the mask and be true to who we are."

JIN

"I have a motto of my life, 'If you behave young, your face becomes young, too.'"

JUNGKOOK

"When I was younger, I thought that everything would just come to me eventually, but now I see I have to take the initiative and practice to improve myself."

V

"I am not scared of looking ugly. And I'm thankful that [my fans] like me even when I make weird facial expressions. I don't plan on looking handsome in an unnatural way. That would be a burden."

J-HOPE

"Jimin is usually really cute. In other words, he was born with cuteness."

ALL THE ANSWERS

Are You Their No. 1 Fan?
Pages 6–8

1.	c	4.	a	7.	a	10.	a
2.	c	5.	b	8.	c	11.	c
3.	c	6.	b	9.	b	12.	c

Fact File: RM
Page 9
The fib is fact number three

Find The Tune
Pages 10–11

F	M	O	T	W	U	H	K	S	E	C	P	R	L	D
B	R	M	E	N	O	M	R	O	H	F	O	R	A	W
P	C	J	A	G	I	S	T	G	U	Y	H	E	P	S
R	U	S	X	E	M	I	C	R	O	P	V	I	N
N	P	H	E	F	R	D	O	X	A	J	A	W	T	E
S	M	Y	E	A	R	Q	R	S	F	X	M	D	Z	R
D	J	O	V	K	L	U	E	B	B	V	C	I	S	I
B	W	Z	O	E	T	O	X	R	Y	T	A	E	P	E
I	S	I	L	V	E	R	S	P	O	O	N	R	R	K
T	C	G	E	P	R	I	D	F	B	M	K	P	I	D
M	S	J	K	H	O	W	E	P	D	E	Q	Z	N	B
L	E	A	A	T	K	T	V	G	O	B	I	N	G	O
N	N	O	F	Y	R	I	P	S	P	U	T	W	D	R
L	W	S	A	V	E	M	E	C	E	H	I	L	A	C
N	R	E	V	U	L	N	I	Y	O	B	D	J	Y	P

Celebrity Love
Pages 12–14

1.	Liam Payne	7.	John Legend	11.	Jared Leto
2.	Meghan Trainor	8.	The Chainsmokers	12.	Shawn Mendes
3.	Camila Cabello			13.	Halsey
4.	John Cena	9.	Tyra Banks	14.	Kehlani
5.	Peter Crouch	10.	Backstreet Boys	15.	Charlie Puth
6.	Taylor Swift			16.	Ansel Elgort

Fact File: Jin
Page 19
The fib is fact number one

Who Said It?
Pages 20–21

1.	Jimin	4.	J-Hope	7.	Jin
2.	V	5.	RM	8.	RM
3.	Suga	6.	Jungkoook		

Spot The Fakes
Pages 22–24

1.	True	6.	True	11.	False
2.	True	7.	True	12.	False
3.	False	8.	True	13.	True
4.	True	9.	True	14.	True
5.	False	10.	True	15.	True

Mystery Tweeter
Page 25
The mystery Tweeter is Jimin

Fact File: Suga
Page 30
The fib is fact number one

Sharing The Love
Pages 31–33

1. Beautiful
2. Traveling
3. Past
4. Cream
5. Handsome
6. Computer
7. Loved
8. Forest
9. Restaurant
10. Jokes
11. Bed
12. Drying
13. Pants

Crack That Crossword
Pages 34–35

Fact File: J-Hope
Page 40
The fib is fact number two

Mystery Tweeter
Page 45
The mystery Tweeter is Jin

Fact File: Jimin
Page 46
The fib is fact number one

Spot The Difference
In Picture Section

1. V's shirt is missing 'BURBERRYS'

2. Suga's blazer has an extra button

3. Suga is missing an earring

4. Jin is missing the stripes on the cuff of his shirt

5. Jungkook's jumper has an added red patch

6. RM's lips are purple

7. Jimin's tie is missing a flower

8. J-Hope has an extra ring on his right hand

Mystery Tweeter
Page 49
The mystery Tweeter is J-Hope

Crack That Crossword
Pages 54–55

Mystery Tweeter
Page 56
The mystery Tweeter is Jungkook

Tour-Time Teaser
Pages 57–58

1. "No More Dream"
2. "We Are Bulletproof Pt. 2"
3. "Danger"
4. "War of Hormone"
5. "Boy in Luv"
6. "Blood Sweat & Tears"
7. "Fire"
8. "Fake Love"
9. "Dope"
10. "DNA"
11. "Save Me"
12. "Mic Drop"

Fact File: V
Page 59
The fib is fact number four

Shhh!
Pages 60–62

1. Jimin
2. V
3. Jungkook
4. Suga
5. J-Hope
6. V
7. V
8. RM
9. Jin
10. Jin
11. RM
12. Suga

Mystery Tweeter
Page 63
The mystery Tweeter is RM

Mystery Tweeter
Page 71
The mystery Tweeter is Suga

Fact File: Jungkook
Page 75
The fib is fact number two

Secret Gig
Page 79
The gig is taking place in: Gwangju
The special guest is: Ariana Grande

Helping Hands
Pages 80–81

1. Rice
2. Love Myself
3. Jimin
4. Suga
5. Ice Bucket
6. 2014
7. Love Food Bank
8. V and Jimin

Mystery Tweeter
Page 82
The mystery Tweeter is V